OmniBook Ultra

Power, Portability, or Just a Compromise?

An Analytical Dive into HP's Latest High-Performance Laptop—for Tech Enthusiasts, Professionals, and Savvy Shoppers

Joe E. Grayson

Table of Contents

Introduction

HP's Spectre series has long held a distinguished place in the laptop world, earning a reputation for combining premium build quality, top-tier performance, and a design that stands out in both style and substance. The Spectre models weren't just about technical power; they symbolized HP's commitment to delivering a seamless experience for professionals and creatives alike who valued both aesthetics and functionality. The Spectre 14, in particular, set high standards, embodying an approach that balanced design finesse with high-performance specs, effectively establishing itself as a favorite among premium Windows laptops.

In comes the OmniBook Ultra, a new face that, at first glance, seems poised to carry on the

Spectre's legacy but takes a different approach, introducing a mix of intrigue and skepticism. The OmniBook Ultra isn't marketed as a direct successor to the Spectre series but rather as a new contender in the high-performance segment. It's positioned as a workhorse aimed at professionals who need strong CPU power and broad application compatibility, especially those in fields like programming or audio engineering. Unlike the Spectre, which drew attention with its luxurious finishes and refined elements, the OmniBook Ultra appears to lean toward a more practical approach, focusing on delivering performance for users with specific productivity needs rather than appealing solely to those who value the aesthetics and polish that defined the Spectre line.

This shift in focus raises a central question: does the OmniBook Ultra genuinely fulfill the promise of a premium experience, or does it make compromises that might leave certain users wanting more? By stepping back from some of the features that defined its predecessors, HP seems to be testing the balance between power and polish. With the OmniBook Ultra, they may be signaling a shift toward prioritizing functionality over the frills that typically come with high-end models. This exploration aims to uncover whether HP has successfully met the needs of performance-focused users or if the sacrifices made in design, display, and other features ultimately limit its appeal in the premium market.

As we examine the OmniBook Ultra in detail, this underlying question persists, inviting a closer look into the core of what it offers.

Chapter 1: First Impressions and Design Aesthetics

The design of the OmniBook Ultra immediately sets it apart from its predecessors in the Spectre series, which were known for their polished finishes and meticulous attention to detail. Where the Spectre series often showcased sleek, bold aesthetics with a sense of luxury, the OmniBook Ultra takes a distinctly minimalist approach, giving it a simpler, more utilitarian look. Its color scheme leans toward neutral tones, and without the elegant flourishes or reflective accents that made the Spectre models stand out, it lacks that instant visual impact. Instead, the OmniBook Ultra appears as if it's built for those who prioritize a straightforward, no-nonsense approach in a laptop, catering to individuals who might place more emphasis on functionality than on owning a visually striking device.

When it comes to build quality, the OmniBook Ultra is clearly designed to withstand regular, intensive use. The materials feel sturdy and durable, suggesting that this laptop can handle the wear and tear of daily professional tasks without issue. However, this durability comes at a cost: compared to the lighter, more agile feel of the Spectre models, the OmniBook Ultra feels heavier in hand. At about 100 grams more than its predecessor, it sacrifices the feather-light appeal of premium ultrabooks for a more substantial, almost rugged presence. It's as if HP has built a tool meant to be reliable above all, emphasizing sturdiness over sleekness.

For many users, the OmniBook Ultra's weight might not seem particularly significant at first, but in a category filled with increasingly lightweight options, every gram counts. This device's extra heft might make it feel more secure during use, but it also detracts from the convenience factor that many expect from a premium 14-inch laptop. In essence, the OmniBook Ultra feels like it's built to last, much like a trusted tool in a professional's arsenal, yet it lacks that sense of effortless refinement. For users drawn to the Spectre's seamless fusion of style and substance, the OmniBook Ultra's design may appear a step back, a shift that will be polarizing depending on one's priorities in a laptop.

The practicality of the OmniBook Ultra's design reveals itself in several ways that may impact the overall user experience, depending on how much convenience and accessibility matter to the user. One of the first notable aspects is the stiffness of its hinges. While the hinges are solid and feel durable, they are far from the smooth, one-handed operation seen on other premium laptops. Users who are accustomed to easily flipping open their laptops with minimal effort may find it frustrating to have to use both hands to lift the screen. For some, this rigidity might be a plus, especially when using the touchscreen, as the stable hinge keeps the screen steady during taps and swipes. However, for others, it's an unnecessary hindrance that detracts from the fluidity of using the device in quick, on-the-go settings.

Another practical consideration is the OmniBook Ultra's limited selection of ports, which may be disappointing given its larger size. The laptop provides only two USB-C ports (both on the same side), a USB-A port, and a headphone jack. This configuration can be restrictive, especially for users accustomed to the versatility of having ports on either side for convenient charging or connecting devices without crowding one side of the laptop. The decision to cluster the USB-C ports on a single side also reduces flexibility, potentially leading to situations where cables become entangled or awkwardly stretched across the workspace. For a laptop aimed at professionals who often connect multiple peripherals, this port limitation might be a significant drawback, especially compared to other models in its price range that offer a more extensive range of options.

Finally, the OmniBook Ultra's larger bezels around the screen are another practical aspect that may feel outdated in the current market. These wider borders give the laptop a bulkier look, which not only affects the overall aesthetic but also reduces the screen-to-body ratio, resulting in a smaller visible display area. In a world where sleek, almost borderless screens have become the standard, the OmniBook Ultra's bezels make it feel like a throwback, a choice that may not sit well with users seeking the immersive, edge-to-edge viewing experience typically associated with premium laptops.

Together, these design decisions suggest that while the OmniBook Ultra has been crafted with durability and functionality in mind, it misses the mark in some areas of convenience and modern appeal. For users focused on pure performance, these might be minor inconveniences, but for those expecting an intuitive, fluid experience, these practical drawbacks may make it feel like a compromise rather than a refined choice.

Chapter 2: Display Matters—A Step Back or a New Direction?

The OmniBook Ultra's display marks a distinct shift from the vibrant OLED screens featured in the Spectre series to a more subdued IPS panel. OLED displays, like those on the Spectre models, are celebrated for their deep contrast, rich color saturation, and ability to produce true blacks by individually illuminating each pixel. This feature results in remarkable color accuracy and a visually immersive experience, especially when viewing high-definition content or working with visually demanding tasks like graphic design. For those who value striking visuals, OLED has been a key part of what makes Spectre models feel high-end and polished.

On the other hand, the OmniBook Ultra's IPS display offers a more practical, durable approach, with distinct benefits of its own, especially for those who plan to use the laptop extensively for varied tasks. IPS panels are known for their consistency, providing stable colors and brightness regardless of viewing angle. Unlike OLED, IPS screens are less susceptible to burn-in, a phenomenon where prolonged display of static images can cause ghosting effects on the screen over time. This durability aspect makes the IPS display better suited to daily productivity tasks or prolonged use, especially for those who may leave certain applications open for extended periods. However, the trade-off is noticeable in color vibrancy and contrast. Where the OLED display in the Spectre could render colors with a certain richness and depth, the IPS panel on the OmniBook appears more muted, with colors that don't quite reach the same levels of intensity.

Beyond the panel type, the OmniBook Ultra's display has a 60 Hz refresh rate and a resolution of 2.2K, both of which reflect certain limitations compared to other high-performance displays. For casual viewers, the 60 Hz refresh rate may seem adequate, as it provides a smooth enough experience for standard web browsing, productivity tasks, and watching videos. However, tech enthusiasts who are used to faster refresh rates, particularly gamers or video editors, may find it lacking. Higher refresh rates, like 120 Hz or 144 Hz, allow for smoother motion and more responsive screen transitions, which can significantly enhance user experience in fast-paced applications. The OmniBook's 60 Hz limit means it won't provide that extra fluidity, making it less appealing to those who value a heightened sense of responsiveness.

In terms of resolution, the 2.2K display is noticeably lower than the 2.8K resolution found on the Spectre. While this reduction may seem minimal on paper, it can impact the clarity of finer details, such as small text or intricate visuals, which may not appear as crisp. For those accustomed to ultra-high-definition screens, the difference in resolution is noticeable, particularly in tasks that demand precision. However, the slightly lower resolution does come with an upside: it conserves battery life. Higher resolutions require more power, so by opting for 2.2K, HP ensures that the OmniBook Ultra can sustain a longer battery life, a feature likely to appeal to users who prioritize endurance over pixel density.

In balancing these display choices, the OmniBook Ultra seems to favor durability and practical functionality over visual allure. It's a setup that appeals to users who need a reliable screen for daily tasks without the bells and whistles of an OLED. While the display may feel like a step down from the Spectre's vivid visuals, it speaks to a different audience, one that values longevity and power efficiency over the finer points of screen technology. For professionals focused on productivity, these compromises might be acceptable, but for those seeking the cinematic quality offered by OLED, the OmniBook's display might feel somewhat understated.

In real-world use, the OmniBook Ultra's screen provides a mixed experience that balances functionality with some noticeable limitations, particularly for those accustomed to premium displays. For day-to-day tasks, the 2.2K resolution is adequate; documents, spreadsheets, and web browsing all look clear enough for general productivity. However, when it comes to small text or intricate visuals, the lower resolution compared to the Spectre's 2.8K display does become apparent. Small text lacks the sharpness one might expect from a high-end laptop, especially when working with detailed documents or reading for extended periods. This slightly reduced clarity might lead some users to adjust font sizes or zoom in more often, which may not be ideal for those who rely on crisp visuals as part of their workflow.

Color vibrancy is another area where the OmniBook Ultra's IPS display may not quite meet the expectations of users familiar with the Spectre's OLED richness. While the IPS panel maintains consistent color accuracy across different viewing angles, its color depth lacks the immersive quality of an OLED screen. Colors appear more muted, especially in high-saturation applications like photo or video editing, where precise color reproduction is crucial. For users who primarily need the laptop for standard tasks, such as coding, text-based work, or even light media consumption, this won't be a significant drawback. However, for creative professionals or those who are used to the vibrant hues and deep contrasts of OLED, the IPS panel can feel somewhat lackluster.

Despite these visual compromises, the screen is functional and practical, and for many users, it doesn't detract from the OmniBook Ultra's usability. The IPS technology ensures that colors remain steady regardless of how the screen is angled, making it useful for situations where multiple people may need to view the screen simultaneously or when working in flexible environments. This stability is an advantage over OLED, which, while vivid, can lose color accuracy from certain angles and is more prone to screen burn-in. Additionally, the modest resolution helps conserve battery life, which means that even though it sacrifices some visual sharpness, it adds value in terms of endurance—a trade-off many users focused on productivity will appreciate.

Overall, while the OmniBook Ultra's display might not inspire awe in users looking for ultra-crisp or vibrant visuals, it is more than adequate for users who prioritize reliability and practicality over visual opulence. For those needing a straightforward and dependable screen to support their daily tasks, this display does the job. But for users who place a premium on visual clarity and color vibrancy, the OmniBook's display might feel like it falls short, reminding them of the compromises made in pursuit of a more utilitarian focus.

Chapter 3: Keyboard and Trackpad—The Input Experience

The keyboard on the OmniBook Ultra introduces a noticeable shift in typing experience, especially for those familiar with the comfortable and responsive feel of the Spectre's keyboard. HP's Spectre series was lauded for its tactile, high-quality keyboard that made typing feel natural, with keys offering a satisfying amount of travel and feedback. This setup catered to long hours of typing, providing a sense of cushion beneath each key press that kept fatigue at bay, even during extended work sessions. The OmniBook Ultra, however, departs from this standard, adopting a "low-travel" key design that feels shallower and firmer.

Typing on the OmniBook Ultra feels distinctly different. The low-travel keys provide less physical feedback, making each press feel firmer and more abrupt, with less of the "give" that Spectre users may be accustomed to. This lower key travel can create a faster typing experience in theory, as fingers don't need to press as deeply for each keystroke. However, the shallow nature of the keys may be less forgiving over time, especially for users who prefer a softer landing for their fingertips. Typing for extended periods on this keyboard may lead to fatigue more quickly than on the Spectre, as users experience the sensation of "bottoming out" with each key press—a result of the limited key depth.

Despite this firmer feel, the keyboard on the OmniBook Ultra has a few redeeming qualities that may appeal to some users. The backlighting, for example, is improved over the Spectre's, with less light bleed around the edges of each key. This backlighting refinement makes it easier to see individual characters in dim environments, allowing for a more focused typing experience without the visual distraction of excess light. However, this improvement may not be enough to satisfy users who value the cushioned, more comfortable feel that the Spectre offered.

For those who rely heavily on a laptop's keyboard for daily work, the OmniBook's keyboard may feel serviceable but lacks the comfort and refinement that Spectre users have come to expect. While the OmniBook's low-travel design may suit some users, especially those accustomed to firmer, more compact keyboards, it doesn't quite reach the level of comfort that high-end ultrabooks typically aim for. In sum, the keyboard is functional and straightforward but represents one of the compromises that HP has made in its transition from the Spectre's luxury-focused design to the more utilitarian build of the

OmniBook Ultra. For users who prioritize comfort in their typing experience, this keyboard may feel like a step back, underscoring the OmniBook Ultra's focus on durability and practicality over the premium touch.

The OmniBook Ultra's transition from a haptic trackpad, as seen in the Spectre series, to a more traditional mechanical trackpad marks a clear departure in terms of usability and finesse. In the Spectre models, the haptic trackpad provided a refined, tactile experience that simulated the feel of pressing down on the pad without any actual movement. This innovation allowed for smoother, more precise control, making it feel effortless and responsive to even the lightest touch. The haptic trackpad was not just a point-and-click tool but an extension of the user's hand, able to discern between intentional actions and accidental brushes of the palm with impressive accuracy.

The OmniBook Ultra, however, features a mechanical trackpad, which brings a more conventional approach that lacks the sophistication of the haptic system. A mechanical trackpad physically clicks when pressed, and while it performs its function effectively, it does not offer the same subtle feedback that a haptic trackpad provides. In practice, this trackpad feels solid and dependable, like a well-worn tool that you can count on to get the job done, but without the elegant touch and sensitivity that the Spectre's trackpad offered. This shift may not be a deal-breaker for everyone, but it's noticeable for users accustomed to the seamless experience provided by haptic feedback.

One of the key areas where this difference is felt is in palm rejection. The Spectre's haptic trackpad had built-in technology that could accurately differentiate between an intentional touch and an accidental graze, particularly important when working in cramped spaces or while typing. The OmniBook's mechanical trackpad, while sturdy, isn't as adept in this regard. It's more likely to pick up on unintended touches, which can cause disruptions for users who rely heavily on trackpad precision. This can be particularly frustrating during activities like editing, where even minor errors in tracking can lead to a break in focus.

Think of the OmniBook Ultra's trackpad as a dependable, rugged tool—a bit like a trusty wrench. It's sturdy, reliable, and functional, getting the job done with straightforward mechanics. However, it lacks the precision instruments' grace and adaptability that can anticipate finer details and deliver a smoother experience. For some users, this trackpad will work perfectly fine, offering reliability without the delicate handling of a haptic system. But for those accustomed to the nuanced experience of a haptic trackpad, the mechanical version on the OmniBook may feel like a regression, emphasizing practicality over polish.

Chapter 4: Performance Unleashed—Powerhouse or Power-Hungry?

The heart of the OmniBook Ultra lies in its powerhouse AMD Ryzen 9 HX375 processor, a choice that positions this laptop firmly within the realm of high-performance devices. AMD's Ryzen 9 HX375 is designed for heavy-duty tasks, delivering impressive power and efficiency that cater directly to users who require substantial processing capabilities. This processor's architecture is built on AMD's advanced Zen 5 technology, featuring a balanced mix of high-performance cores that are ideal for managing intensive applications and multitasking environments. It boasts a combination of both performance and efficiency cores, allowing the laptop to dynamically allocate power depending on the workload. This translates into faster speeds when pushing the laptop's limits and a more conservative power draw for everyday tasks, balancing efficiency with raw power.

For professionals dealing with demanding tasks—whether it's compiling code, processing large datasets, or working with complex audio projects—the Ryzen 9 HX375 delivers performance that stands out. In benchmark tests like Geekbench, which evaluate real-world CPU performance, the OmniBook Ultra's Ryzen processor ranks among the top performers in its class. This level of capability is particularly appealing to users who need reliability and speed, allowing them to move smoothly through workflows that might otherwise slow down on a less capable system. Unlike many standard CPUs found in consumer laptops, the Ryzen 9 HX375 is tuned to handle complex processing needs without faltering, providing consistent performance even under pressure.

One of the processor's most notable strengths is its compatibility across a broad spectrum of applications. Unlike laptops running on Snapdragon processors or those geared toward lightweight tasks, the OmniBook Ultra with its AMD Ryzen processor maintains compatibility with a wide range of software. This versatility is crucial for professionals like programmers, who may need to run various development environments and virtual machines, or audio engineers, who often rely on specialized software suites. Unlike certain ARM-based systems that can run into compatibility issues with legacy applications, the AMD Ryzen 9 provides a stable, flexible foundation that handles diverse workloads without any hassle.

For users working in technical fields, this compatibility ensures they can rely on the OmniBook Ultra for their daily tasks, knowing that the software they depend on will run smoothly. Programmers benefit from the processor's power to compile code faster, test applications without delay, and seamlessly handle multiple windows and processes. Audio engineers, on the other hand, can take advantage of the laptop's ability to run complex digital audio workstations (DAWs) and plug-ins without the typical slowdown that plagues weaker systems. This broad compatibility not only expands the laptop's appeal but also makes it a smart investment for professionals who need a tool they can rely on across various platforms and applications.

The Ryzen 9 HX375 turns the OmniBook Ultra into a highly versatile machine that doesn't just meet performance expectations—it exceeds them, particularly for users focused on productivity. Its architecture, built to deliver a combination of speed and efficiency, makes it an ideal choice for those who need more than just basic processing power. In a market filled with compromises, the OmniBook's processor choice reflects a clear focus on serious performance, promising users a robust, compatible system that supports demanding tasks across the board.

The OmniBook Ultra's impressive power comes with a high power draw, akin to an engine built for speed that requires precise handling to maintain its peak performance. The AMD Ryzen 9 HX375 processor at the laptop's core is engineered to deliver top-tier speeds, pulling significant power to sustain the heavy processing demands placed on it. During high-intensity tasks, the OmniBook Ultra can feed up to 48 watts of power to the CPU, allowing it to tackle resource-heavy applications head-on and deliver consistently fast results. However, as with any powerful engine, this high power draw comes with the challenge of managing the resulting heat, which, if left unchecked, can impact both performance and comfort during extended use.

HP has equipped the OmniBook Ultra with a thermal management system that acts as a control mechanism for this high-power engine. The system's goal is to maintain a balance between the power needed to drive high-performance tasks and the cooling necessary to prevent overheating. Just as a high-performance car engine relies on a cooling system to avoid overheating, the OmniBook's processor is supported by a cooling setup that steps in to prevent the laptop from becoming excessively hot. This setup includes strategically placed fans and heat pipes designed to channel warmth away from critical components, ensuring that the laptop can sustain its performance without compromising on longevity.

Even with this system in place, the OmniBook's power-focused design means that it does generate noticeable warmth during intensive tasks, and users can sometimes feel the heat radiate through the keyboard or base. For brief bursts of high performance, such as compiling code or rendering large files, the thermal management can keep the laptop stable. But in prolonged, continuous workloads, the OmniBook's thermal system must work harder, and at times it may limit the processor's peak speed to maintain manageable temperatures. This is much like easing off the gas pedal in a car to prevent the engine from overheating on a long, steep climb; the laptop may temporarily throttle performance to cool down, ensuring that it doesn't run at unsustainable levels.

In lighter tasks, however, the OmniBook's thermal system keeps the laptop cool and quiet, with fans that rarely spin up to distracting levels. This means that for day-to-day productivity and casual use, the heat is well-contained and barely noticeable. It's only when the laptop is pushed to its full potential that the balance of power and heat management becomes more apparent. For users who value a high-performance machine and understand the trade-off of dealing with occasional warmth, the OmniBook Ultra's thermal management system does a solid job. Yet, like any high-speed engine, it requires a measure of thoughtful handling to get the best out of it without pushing it beyond its limits. This balance between power and control is what makes the OmniBook Ultra both exciting and unique—a laptop that offers remarkable speed with the understanding that managing heat is part of the experience.

Chapter 5: Graphics Capabilities—Integrated GPU Limits and Gaming Potential

The OmniBook Ultra's integrated GPU is built to handle a range of visual tasks with efficiency, yet it inherently differs from a dedicated GPU setup in both power and capability. Integrated GPUs, like the one in the OmniBook Ultra, are part of the laptop's main processor, allowing them to handle basic graphic tasks without consuming significant power or space. This setup makes the OmniBook Ultra well-suited to everyday tasks, from video playback to photo editing, all while preserving battery life. Integrated graphics are also less demanding on a laptop's thermal management system, making them a practical choice for lightweight, thin laptops.

However, when compared to a dedicated GPU, which is a standalone component designed specifically for handling intensive graphics, integrated graphics are limited in performance. Dedicated GPUs, such as those found in gaming laptops or high-end workstations, have more processing cores and memory bandwidth, enabling them to handle complex visual effects, high-resolution rendering, and demanding video or image processing tasks with ease. They are preferred by gamers, visual artists, and video editors who require powerful graphical capabilities for detailed, resource-intensive work. The OmniBook's integrated GPU, while capable, falls short of delivering the full visual power that these dedicated GPUs provide, meaning it isn't suited for high-end gaming or 3D modeling tasks.

In terms of gaming, the limitations of an integrated GPU become apparent, especially with the OmniBook Ultra's 60 Hz refresh rate cap. This restriction means that while the laptop can run games at acceptable frame rates, the display can only refresh up to 60 frames per second. For casual or non-demanding games, like League of Legends, the OmniBook Ultra's integrated GPU handles gameplay smoothly enough at medium-to-high settings. The laptop manages to maintain a steady frame rate that makes the game playable, with reasonable visuals and responsiveness. However, this 60 Hz limit creates a bottleneck, as more graphically intense games or high-frame-rate settings are out of reach.

For example, while League of Legends might run comfortably, gamers used to higher refresh rates, like 120 Hz or 144 Hz, will notice the difference.

Faster refresh rates allow for smoother transitions and more responsive controls, making gameplay feel immersive and allowing players to react more swiftly to in-game events. The OmniBook's 60 Hz cap means that the action feels slightly slower and less fluid, particularly in moments of rapid on-screen movement. For gamers accustomed to ultra-smooth visuals, this cap may reduce gaming enjoyment, as it limits the level of immersion and responsiveness the laptop can provide.

Ultimately, the OmniBook Ultra's integrated GPU is ideal for users who need dependable, moderate graphics performance without the demands of high-frame-rate gaming or detailed 3D rendering. For those seeking a machine that supports extensive graphical work or immersive gaming, a dedicated GPU would offer a more suitable and powerful experience. The OmniBook

Ultra's setup is a solid choice for casual gamers and professionals focused on productivity, but it isn't intended to match the immersive capabilities of dedicated GPU systems, making it a versatile yet limited choice in the world of graphics.

The OmniBook Ultra's integrated GPU is designed with a certain kind of user in mind—someone who needs reliable, moderate graphics performance without the demands of high-end gaming or intensive 3D work. It's ideal for those who occasionally enjoy lighter gaming or need to run graphics-focused applications as part of their work but don't require the power or complexity of a dedicated GPU setup. This laptop's graphics capabilities are suited for users who prioritize productivity and versatility, especially those who see gaming as a secondary activity rather than a primary focus.

For casual gamers, the OmniBook's integrated GPU offers enough power to handle popular, less demanding titles like League of Legends, Rocket League, or even some RPGs, as long as they're comfortable with medium to high settings instead of ultra or max. The 60 Hz refresh rate cap and the integrated GPU together mean that while these games will run smoothly, they won't reach the level of immersive fluidity that higher-end gaming machines with dedicated GPUs can offer. Users who are content with stable frame rates and solid visuals, rather than the latest high-frame-rate or graphically intensive experiences, will find the OmniBook's GPU more than adequate for enjoyable gameplay.

The OmniBook Ultra is also well-suited for users who rely on graphics performance for work, like those who may occasionally edit photos, render basic 3D models, or produce presentations that involve some visual processing. The integrated GPU handles these tasks efficiently without draining excessive power or heating up, balancing performance with practical functionality. For these users, the OmniBook provides a capable, power-conscious solution that meets most professional needs without the extra heat and battery drain of a dedicated GPU.

In essence, the OmniBook's GPU is for the professional who occasionally games, the creative who dips into graphics, or the productivity-focused user who wants reliable visual performance without the added cost or complexity of a gaming-oriented system. This graphics setup is a dependable choice for those who need more than just basic visuals but don't need the specialized capabilities of a dedicated GPU, positioning the OmniBook Ultra as a versatile yet efficient option in the laptop market.

Chapter 6: Portability and Battery Life—Balancing Power and Practicality

The OmniBook Ultra offers impressive battery life when handling everyday tasks, making it a reliable choice for users who spend much of their time on light activities like browsing, streaming, word processing, and general productivity. In such scenarios, the laptop can run for extended periods—up to 16 hours in video playback tests—without needing a recharge. This longevity is due, in part, to its moderate 2.2K resolution display, which draws less power than higher-resolution screens, allowing the battery to stretch further. For users who prioritize endurance and need a laptop that can keep up with long days of moderate use, the OmniBook's battery life is a significant asset, adding to its appeal as a practical, portable work device.

However, when the OmniBook Ultra is pushed into performance-intensive tasks, such as running complex software, multitasking heavily, or playing games, the demands on the battery increase, and the longevity noticeably decreases. Under these circumstances, the laptop's processor and integrated GPU draw more power to maintain performance, and the battery life drops accordingly. While it can handle bursts of high-intensity tasks, the OmniBook is most efficient and long-lasting when used for lighter, less demanding activities. Users relying on the laptop for consistent high-performance applications may find themselves needing to plug in sooner to maintain that level of power.

The OmniBook Ultra also adapts its power usage when unplugged, scaling back its energy consumption to conserve battery. This adjustment works like a high-powered engine that switches gears when it's off the charger, allowing the laptop to sustain a respectable level of performance without draining the battery too quickly. When unplugged, the OmniBook reduces its power draw and may slightly limit the processor's speed to maintain a balance between performance and endurance. While it doesn't compromise heavily on capability, this shift is enough to keep battery consumption in check, ensuring the laptop can still perform moderately demanding tasks without an immediate need to reconnect to a power source.

In essence, the OmniBook Ultra is designed to provide flexibility, functioning as both a high-performance machine when plugged in and a battery-conscious device when running on its internal power. This intelligent power scaling makes it a versatile tool for users who need extended battery life for routine tasks but also value the ability to switch to higher performance when connected to a power source. For professionals balancing between mobility and performance, this adaptive power management offers a practical solution, ensuring the OmniBook Ultra remains efficient and reliable across varying usage demands.

The OmniBook Ultra's port selection presents a blend of practicality and limitations, particularly when compared to other high-performance laptops in its category, such as the MacBook Pro 14. The OmniBook offers a basic array of connectivity options, including two USB-C ports with Thunderbolt support, a single USB-A port, and a headphone jack. While this setup provides a degree of versatility, it doesn't quite match the extensive port offerings found on other premium models, which can be a drawback for users who rely on multiple external devices.

One notable inconvenience is that both USB-C ports are located on the same side of the laptop. For many users, this layout can prove restrictive, as it limits flexibility in arranging cables and connected devices. Charging from the right side only, for instance, means that the power cord could end up crossing over or crowding the workspace in certain settings, especially in environments where space is tight. The presence of only one USB-A port also means users may find themselves needing a dongle or adapter more frequently, particularly for connecting legacy devices or peripherals without USB-C compatibility. For professionals with an extensive array of external devices, such as keyboards, external drives, or multiple monitors, this limited port selection can hinder productivity by requiring additional accessories.

In comparison, the MacBook Pro 14 stands out with a more comprehensive port lineup, which includes an HDMI port, an SD card slot, and multiple Thunderbolt ports positioned on both sides of the laptop. This broader selection allows MacBook Pro users to connect to a wider variety of devices without needing adapters and offers more flexibility for creative and professional workflows. The MacBook's setup supports high-resolution external displays, streamlined media transfers via the SD card slot, and the convenience of plugging in on either side, making it a preferred choice for users who value seamless connectivity.

For the OmniBook Ultra, the limited port configuration may work well enough for light or moderate users, particularly those who don't require extensive peripheral support on a daily basis. However, for power users or professionals who need to switch between multiple devices, display options, or storage solutions, the OmniBook's port selection may feel restrictive. The laptop's connectivity limitations are ultimately a trade-off in favor of its slim, portable design, yet it's a compromise that could impact productivity for users accustomed to more comprehensive port setups. In this sense, the OmniBook's port selection reflects its design priorities, catering to a more minimalistic user profile while leaving certain professionals wanting for additional connectivity options.

Chapter 7: Sound and Visuals—Speakers, Webcam, and Audio Quality

The OmniBook Ultra's speakers provide an audio experience that covers the essentials but lacks the depth, richness, and power found in competitors like the MacBook Pro. Imagine a basic home speaker system—reliable enough for casual listening but missing the layers of sound and clarity that make music or movies feel immersive. The OmniBook's speakers function in much the same way, delivering clear audio that is suitable for standard tasks like video calls, casual media playback, or listening to background music while working. However, they lack the fullness that would make them stand out as exceptional, especially when compared to the dynamic audio capabilities of the MacBook Pro.

In the MacBook Pro, Apple has incorporated a more advanced speaker system that is known for its depth and spatial audio. With a broader range of sound, enhanced bass, and clear separation between channels, the MacBook's speakers create an almost surround-sound experience, enveloping the listener and bringing out nuances in music, dialogue, and sound effects. It's akin to upgrading from a basic speaker to a finely tuned audio system capable of producing vibrant soundscapes. This difference is particularly noticeable in the bass response and volume levels, where the MacBook's speakers can deliver fuller lows and louder, clearer highs without distortion. For users who value high-quality audio or frequently use their laptop for multimedia, this speaker quality can make a tangible difference.

By contrast, the OmniBook's speakers deliver a straightforward, functional audio output that is clear but lacks the resonance and stereo separation needed for a truly immersive experience. Bass is subdued, making music and cinematic audio sound flatter, and the overall volume capacity is limited, which might require users to connect external speakers or headphones if they need louder or more nuanced sound. This lack of depth means that the OmniBook's audio is serviceable but not remarkable, particularly for users who expect a richer auditory experience in a premium laptop.

In essence, the OmniBook Ultra's speakers do the job well enough for everyday use but don't create the same engaging audio environment that competitors like the MacBook Pro provide. They're like a basic speaker system—suitable for getting the essentials across but without the layers of sound and quality that make audio come alive. For users who prioritize immersive sound, this difference may stand out, underscoring that the OmniBook's strengths lie elsewhere, while audio remains an area of compromise in favor of other design considerations.

The OmniBook Ultra's 1440p webcam offers a level of clarity and detail that stands out among standard laptop webcams, most of which are still capped at 720p or 1080p. This higher resolution makes it particularly suitable for users who rely heavily on video calls and online meetings, where a clear, sharp image can make a significant difference in how one is perceived. The 1440p resolution provides noticeably sharper visuals, capturing details that lesser webcams might blur or obscure, which can be especially beneficial for professionals in fields like remote consulting, online presentations, or any work where high-quality video presence is a priority.

Compared to standard webcams, the OmniBook's 1440p setup delivers better performance in varied lighting conditions, handling shadows and highlights more effectively. This means that even in less-than-ideal lighting, the webcam can maintain a balanced image, avoiding the washed-out or overly dark results often seen in lower-resolution cameras. For users who frequently work in different environments, this versatility helps ensure a consistent, professional appearance on video calls. Additionally, the higher resolution can be an asset for content creators or educators conducting webinars, as it provides the clarity needed to display finer details without the need for an external camera.

In terms of audio quality, however, the OmniBook Ultra's microphone performance is standard, functional but unremarkable. While it captures sound clearly enough for casual meetings, it lacks the noise cancellation and clarity enhancements found in more advanced setups. In environments with background noise, users may need to rely on external microphones to achieve professional-grade audio quality. This is one area where devices like the MacBook Pro or specialized external webcams may still have an edge, offering built-in mics that better handle ambient noise and deliver more consistent sound quality.

Overall, the OmniBook Ultra's 1440p webcam is an asset for users who prioritize video quality and want a clear, professional image without needing to add external equipment. It provides a crisp, well-defined video feed that surpasses the capabilities of typical laptop webcams, making it a valuable feature for those who rely on visual clarity in their daily work or personal connections. While the audio capture remains fairly basic, the high-resolution webcam itself is a definite highlight, offering users a level of visual quality that complements the laptop's professional appeal.

Chapter 8: Target Audience—Who Benefits Most?

The OmniBook Ultra is tailored for professionals who demand strong, reliable performance across a range of applications. Its AMD Ryzen 9 HX375 processor, a high-powered chip designed for versatility, positions the OmniBook as a practical choice for users in technical and creative fields, particularly programmers, engineers, and those whose work relies on the seamless handling of multiple applications. Unlike consumer-focused laptops that prioritize aesthetics or lightweight convenience, the OmniBook Ultra is built to deliver serious computing power, making it ideal for tasks that require sustained performance without compromise.

For programmers, the OmniBook Ultra offers a robust environment for coding, testing, and deploying applications. The AMD processor enables efficient multitasking, allowing users to run development environments, virtual machines, and various tools simultaneously. Its broad compatibility with widely used development platforms and software ensures that programmers can depend on the OmniBook to handle complex workflows without compatibility issues. This laptop's integrated GPU is also capable of running development tools that require some graphical processing, making it a solid option for mobile and web developers who occasionally work with visual elements.

Engineers, particularly those working with data analysis, simulations, or CAD software, will find the OmniBook's processing power advantageous. The Ryzen 9 HX375's multi-core architecture is well-suited for data-intensive applications that benefit from parallel processing, such as engineering simulations or large dataset analyses. The laptop's efficient power management also supports long, uninterrupted work sessions, allowing engineers to maintain productivity without frequent recharging. Moreover, the device's compatibility with Windows and Linux platforms makes it highly adaptable for various engineering software, including technical simulations or modeling applications that require cross-platform support.

One of the key advantages of the AMD processor over Snapdragon-based laptops is its extensive application compatibility. Snapdragon laptops, which typically use ARM-based processors, can run into limitations with legacy or specialized applications, especially those that require x86 architecture support. This constraint can be a significant barrier for professionals working with software that isn't optimized for ARM, as it may either perform poorly or not run at all on Snapdragon devices. By contrast, the AMD Ryzen 9 processor in the OmniBook Ultra provides full compatibility with the x86 ecosystem, ensuring that users have access to the full range of professional applications they rely on without compromise. This makes the OmniBook Ultra a safer choice for professionals who need reliable access to industry-standard tools.

For users in fields that demand both power and compatibility, the OmniBook Ultra stands out as a capable, versatile device. It meets the needs of professionals who require strong computing performance, a high degree of compatibility, and a device that can adapt to various technical workflows without missing a beat. Unlike Snapdragon-based alternatives that are best suited for light, everyday tasks, the OmniBook's

AMD processor makes it a dependable choice for professionals who need more out of their machine, ensuring a smooth experience with both modern and legacy applications. This broad compatibility and processing strength make the OmniBook Ultra an excellent option for technical professionals who value both flexibility and reliability in a high-performance laptop.

For the budget-conscious professional, the OmniBook Ultra represents a unique balance of performance and practicality—what could be called a "premium compromise." This device delivers impressive processing power and broad application compatibility, making it a great choice for those who need a high-performance laptop but aren't focused on the luxury finishings or cutting-edge aesthetics of more expensive models. However, at its full MSRP, typically ranging between $1,500 and $1,700, the

OmniBook Ultra doesn't entirely match the high-end features found in similarly priced competitors, such as OLED screens, ultra-slim bezels, or high-fidelity audio systems.

This is where waiting for a discount can transform the OmniBook Ultra from a capable yet costly device into a smart, value-driven investment. HP frequently offers promotions, and savvy buyers can often find the OmniBook for $300 to $400 off its MSRP. In this discounted range, typically between $1,000 and $1,400, the OmniBook Ultra becomes a more attractive option, as its strengths—powerful AMD processor, extensive compatibility, and efficient thermal management—shine without the expectation of premium extras.

By holding out for a sale, budget-conscious users can avoid paying for full-price frills they may not need, while still gaining access to the OmniBook's top-tier performance. This approach makes the OmniBook Ultra an appealing choice for those who prioritize functionality and reliability over luxurious details. The discounted price provides a better balance, where the laptop's robust capabilities come into sharper focus and feel well worth the investment. For users willing to wait for a deal, the OmniBook Ultra becomes a competitive, high-performance laptop that doesn't compromise on essential features, allowing them to enjoy premium-level processing power without the premium price tag.

Chapter 9: Software Compatibility—Linux and Beyond

Running Linux, specifically Fedora 41 Beta, on the OmniBook Ultra opens up a host of possibilities for users in programming and tech fields, showcasing the laptop's adaptability and compatibility with open-source operating systems. Fedora, known for its robustness and cutting-edge features, installs smoothly on the OmniBook Ultra, providing a stable environment for developers, data scientists, and engineers who rely on Linux for specialized tools and workflows. The experience of running Linux on the OmniBook Ultra is largely seamless, with hardware components such as the trackpad, webcam, speakers, and display adjusting to the new OS without issue. This out-of-the-box compatibility makes the OmniBook Ultra an appealing option for tech professionals who value flexibility in choosing their operating system.

For programmers, the benefits are substantial. Linux provides direct access to tools like the command line, various development environments, and package managers that simplify software installation and management, enhancing productivity. The OmniBook's powerful AMD Ryzen processor pairs well with Linux, allowing for efficient compiling of code, running virtual machines, and managing multiple development environments without lag or resource limitations. With Linux's vast library of open-source software, developers can easily customize their work environment to suit their specific needs, from lightweight setups for scripting and web development to more robust configurations for machine learning and data processing.

Another key advantage for tech professionals is the ease of network management and server connectivity that Linux facilitates. For users working in IT, networking, or cybersecurity, the ability to run native Linux tools makes the OmniBook Ultra a practical choice for tasks such as configuring servers, testing network security, or managing cloud environments. Linux's built-in support for SSH and other networking tools also simplifies the process of remote server access, adding convenience for those who work across multiple systems or locations.

Furthermore, the OmniBook's reliable thermal management and power efficiency ensure that the laptop performs well even during resource-intensive operations. Whether the user is running containerized applications, large-scale simulations, or software development kits, the OmniBook's stability under Linux means that it can sustain these demanding tasks without excessive heating or performance throttling. This performance consistency is a strong advantage for professionals who need a dependable machine that can keep up with high workloads typical in technical fields.

For tech professionals seeking a Linux-compatible laptop with both power and adaptability, the OmniBook Ultra delivers an excellent experience. Its hardware integration with Fedora 41 Beta makes it a solid platform for open-source workflows, and its processor power and application flexibility allow it to handle the rigorous demands of programming, engineering, and IT work. The OmniBook Ultra's ability to smoothly transition into a Linux environment underscores its versatility and positions it as an ideal tool for tech users who value the freedom and control Linux offers in their professional toolkit.

The OmniBook Ultra's hardware compatibility in Linux environments is a significant advantage for open-source enthusiasts who seek a laptop that seamlessly integrates with their preferred operating system. Running Fedora 41 Beta on the OmniBook Ultra showcases the device's readiness to support key components—trackpad, webcam, speakers, and display—without the need for extensive driver adjustments or workarounds, a notable convenience for users familiar with Linux's occasional hardware challenges.

The trackpad on the OmniBook Ultra works smoothly in Fedora, providing a responsive and precise user experience. Gestures such as scrolling, tapping, and multi-finger navigation are supported right out of the box, meaning Linux users can easily navigate and control applications with minimal setup. For developers or professionals who spend long hours on their laptops, having a fully functional trackpad without needing additional configuration is both time-saving and practical, enhancing productivity.

The 1440p webcam, which is above average for laptop webcams, performs well in Linux as well. Its high resolution translates seamlessly, making video conferencing applications like Zoom, Jitsi, and open-source alternatives work effectively. The quality is consistent, capturing clear, sharp visuals, which is beneficial for those who rely on video meetings or create content. Open-source enthusiasts who frequently participate in remote work or virtual collaboration will appreciate the reliable webcam performance without the need for external cameras or hardware adjustments.

The speakers on the OmniBook Ultra also integrate effectively with Linux, delivering clear and balanced audio suitable for calls, media playback, and light editing. While the speakers lack the deep bass or volume found in some competitors, they are consistent across applications, allowing Linux users to enjoy sound without compatibility issues. This smooth integration can be particularly helpful for those using audio editing tools or simply enjoying media in their downtime, as they won't encounter the frustrating audio glitches that can sometimes accompany Linux hardware setups.

Additionally, the display resolution and brightness controls function correctly in Linux, providing users with control over their viewing experience. Fedora 41 Beta easily recognizes the OmniBook's 2.2K display, and users can adjust brightness settings directly from the system, which is especially useful for professionals working in various lighting conditions. The display's color accuracy and viewing angles remain stable, making it well-suited for coding, design, or general productivity tasks.

The OmniBook Ultra's compatibility across these core hardware components makes it an appealing option for open-source enthusiasts who prioritize a smooth Linux experience. Users looking for a laptop that doesn't require manual configurations to fully function will find that the OmniBook Ultra handles Linux integration with ease, allowing them to focus on their work or projects rather than troubleshooting hardware. This high level of compatibility ensures that the OmniBook Ultra stands out as a powerful,

Linux-friendly device that meets the needs of users committed to open-source tools and environments.

Chapter 10: Pricing Reality—Why MSRP Isn't Justified

At its MSRP of $1,500 to $1,700, the OmniBook Ultra's value proposition falls short when compared to other premium laptops offering more refined features at similar price points. While the OmniBook Ultra boasts a powerful AMD Ryzen 9 processor and excellent application compatibility, it lacks some high-end features commonly found in laptops within this price range, such as OLED displays, advanced audio systems, and an extensive port selection. For instance, the MacBook Pro 14 or Dell XPS models, which are often available around the same MSRP, provide premium touches like higher-resolution displays, enhanced color accuracy, superior audio quality, and better build aesthetics, making them feel more aligned with the expectations for a premium device.

In real-world pricing, however, the OmniBook Ultra becomes a much more attractive option when available at a discount. With HP's regular sales and promotions, it's not uncommon to find the OmniBook Ultra for $300 to $400 off its MSRP, bringing it into the $1,000 to $1,400 range. At this reduced price, the OmniBook Ultra's focus on performance becomes a standout feature, delivering significant processing power for users who need robust CPU capabilities without the premium price of luxury add-ons. For professionals who prioritize functionality and reliability over aesthetics or high-end display features, the discounted OmniBook Ultra offers a competitive edge and makes it a more sensible choice.

To help readers find the best deal on the OmniBook Ultra, price tracking tools can be a valuable resource. Sites like CamelCamelCamel (for Amazon listings) or Keepa allow users to monitor price trends over time, helping to identify the right moment to buy. Additionally, price tracking websites such as Slickdeals or Honey can alert users to discounts, flash sales, or bundled deals that make the OmniBook Ultra more affordable. For HP products specifically, signing up for HP's newsletter or checking their website during major sales events—such as Black Friday, Cyber Monday, or back-to-school promotions—can yield substantial savings.

Savvy shoppers may also benefit from comparing prices across multiple retailers and looking into seasonal deals, which often provide the best discounts. Some credit card companies and online shopping platforms offer cashback or price protection policies, which can further enhance the savings when purchasing the OmniBook Ultra at a discounted rate.

Ultimately, waiting for a discount transforms the OmniBook Ultra from a high-priced option with compromises into a well-rounded, budget-friendly powerhouse. By using price trackers and staying informed about retailer promotions, potential buyers can make a budget-conscious choice, securing the OmniBook Ultra's strengths without paying the premium MSRP. This strategy provides the best of both worlds: the performance and compatibility that professionals need, at a price that aligns better with its value.

For those considering the OmniBook Ultra at its full MSRP of $1,500 to $1,700, several alternative laptops provide a more compelling value by offering a blend of performance and premium features that the OmniBook lacks. Among these, the MacBook Pro 14 and HP ProBook PX13 stand out as strong contenders, each bringing unique advantages to the table while sitting within a similar price range. These alternatives better justify their premium pricing by including high-end features, superior design elements, and enhanced functionality that the OmniBook Ultra's minimalist, performance-focused setup doesn't fully match.

The **MacBook Pro 14** is a leading choice for users willing to invest in a well-rounded, premium laptop experience. Apple's latest MacBook Pro models are powered by the M3 Pro chip (or, at discounts, previous M1 Pro or M2 Pro versions), offering impressive processing power, energy efficiency, and seamless integration with the macOS ecosystem. At a similar price point to the OmniBook Ultra, the MacBook Pro 14 includes a vibrant 3024 x 1964 Retina display with rich color accuracy, high brightness, and a 120 Hz refresh rate. This display not only outperforms the

OmniBook's 2.2K IPS panel but also provides an immersive viewing experience for visual professionals and content creators. The MacBook Pro 14's speakers are also industry-leading, producing deep bass, clear highs, and spatial audio that enhances media consumption and video conferencing. Additionally, the MacBook's design includes a wider port selection with HDMI, an SD card slot, multiple Thunderbolt ports, and charging capability on either side, making it a versatile option for professionals who need flexibility without adapters.

Another strong alternative at a similar price point is **HP's ProBook PX13**, a business-oriented laptop that strikes a balance between performance and premium features. Designed with professionals in mind, the ProBook PX13 comes equipped with a sleek, durable chassis, high-resolution display options, and an efficient keyboard that is comfortable for long typing sessions. While not as powerful as the MacBook Pro's M-series processors, the ProBook PX13's Intel Core i7 or AMD Ryzen 7 processors deliver robust performance, capable of handling multitasking and complex applications with ease. The ProBook PX13 also provides a broader selection of ports than the OmniBook Ultra, with multiple USB-C and USB-A ports, an HDMI output, and an optional Smart Card reader for enhanced security—features that make it especially appealing to users in business or IT fields who require connectivity options without the need for extra adapters.

These alternatives offer more than the OmniBook Ultra at MSRP, particularly for those who value a blend of aesthetics, functionality, and premium features alongside high performance. The MacBook Pro 14 is ideal for users who need a high-quality display, superior audio, and an all-around immersive experience, especially those already integrated into the Apple ecosystem. On the other hand, the ProBook PX13 appeals to professionals who need a well-rounded, durable laptop with a balanced mix of connectivity, security features, and strong processing power.

While the OmniBook Ultra excels in performance for its discounted price, at full MSRP, these competitors offer more comprehensive experiences that better justify their premium costs. By investing in either the MacBook Pro 14 or HP ProBook PX13, users gain a laptop that combines power with features and design elements that enhance daily productivity and enjoyment, providing a better long-term value in the premium laptop market.

Conclusion

The OmniBook Ultra stands out as a robust, high-performance laptop aimed at professionals who prioritize functionality and processing power over luxury features. With its AMD Ryzen 9 processor, broad application compatibility, and efficient thermal management, it's well-equipped to handle demanding workloads, from software development to data analysis. This makes it an attractive choice for users in technical fields who need a laptop that can keep pace with complex, multitasking environments. Its impressive battery life during light tasks also ensures it can keep going through long workdays, especially when used for moderate productivity and everyday applications.

However, the OmniBook Ultra does come with notable compromises. Compared to similarly priced premium laptops, it lacks some of the high-end features found in competitors, such as vibrant OLED displays, refined audio systems, and comprehensive port selections. The 2.2K IPS display is practical but doesn't match the crispness or color accuracy of OLED screens, and the integrated GPU, while capable for casual gaming, doesn't deliver the immersive experience of a dedicated GPU. Additionally, the OmniBook's design leans toward functionality rather than aesthetics, missing the sleek elegance of other laptops in the premium market. The limited port configuration and relatively heavy weight for its size further underscore these trade-offs, making it feel less like a true premium device and more like a workhorse built for performance-driven users.

When evaluating whether the OmniBook Ultra is worth the investment, it's essential to consider the user's specific needs and budget. At full MSRP, the OmniBook Ultra competes with laptops that offer more polished features, and for users who prioritize display quality, audio excellence, or a more versatile port selection, alternatives like the MacBook Pro 14 or HP's ProBook PX13 provide better value. However, at a discounted price, the OmniBook Ultra becomes a compelling option for those who need reliable, high-end processing power without paying for premium frills. For budget-conscious professionals focused on performance and compatibility, waiting for a price drop can transform the OmniBook Ultra into a well-rounded, efficient machine that delivers strong value for money.

Looking ahead, HP has the opportunity to refine the OmniBook series, perhaps by incorporating more premium features to make it a well-rounded device that appeals to a broader audience. Enhancements like a higher-resolution display, improved audio, and a more versatile port selection would elevate the OmniBook Ultra to a fully premium level without sacrificing its core strengths. A future model that combines the performance-driven focus of the current OmniBook with the aesthetic and functional polish found in higher-end competitors would create a truly competitive device. With these adjustments, HP could position the OmniBook as a powerful yet refined option, bridging the gap between functionality and the premium experience that today's professional users expect.

www.ingramcontent.com/pod-product-compliance
Lightning Source LLC
LaVergne TN
LVHW051538050326
832903LV00033B/4309